NATIONAL GEOGRAPHI

My Cat and I

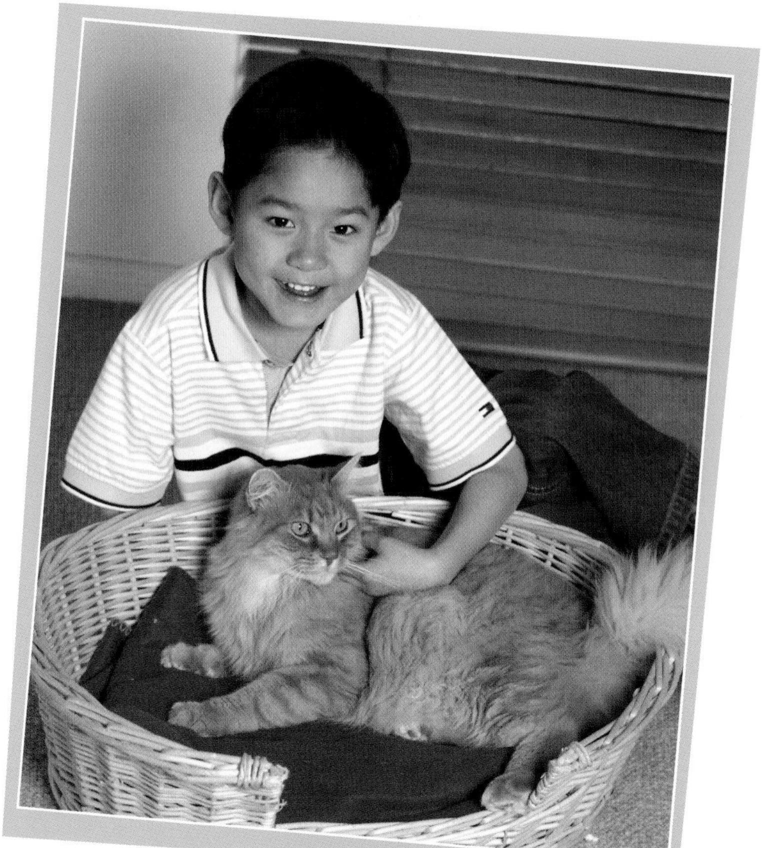

Regina Schirmer

My cat has two eyes.

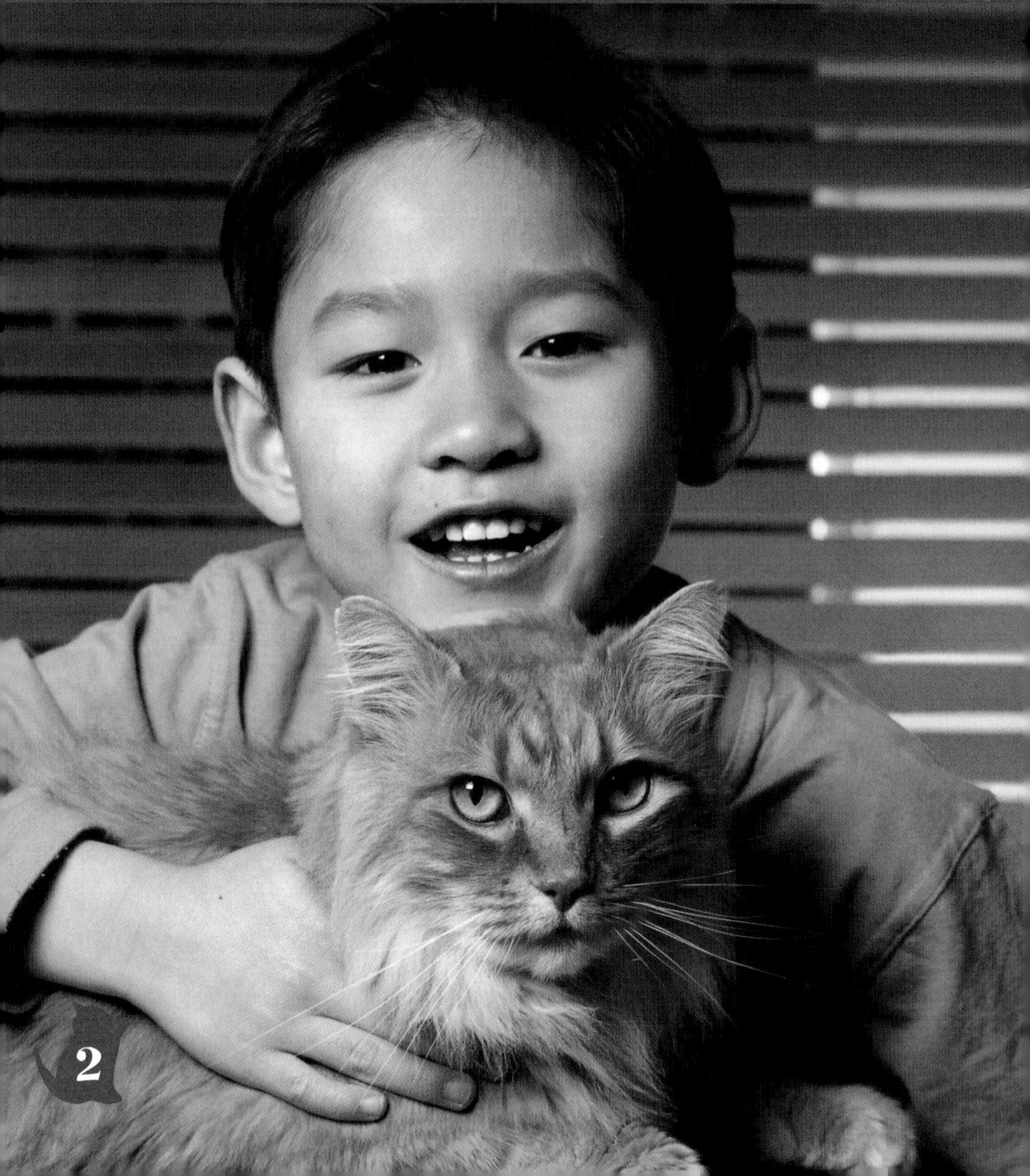

So do I.

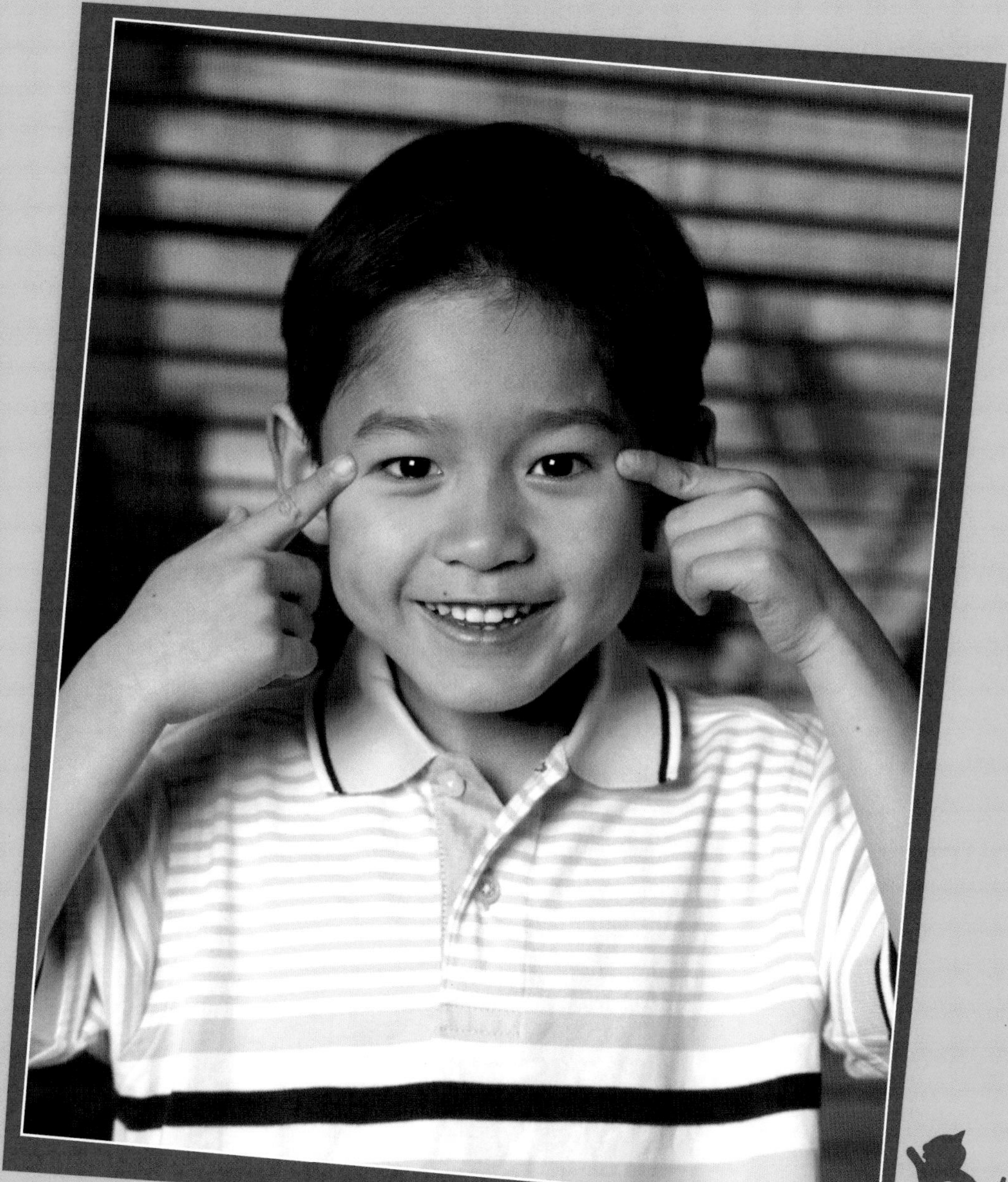

My cat has two ears.

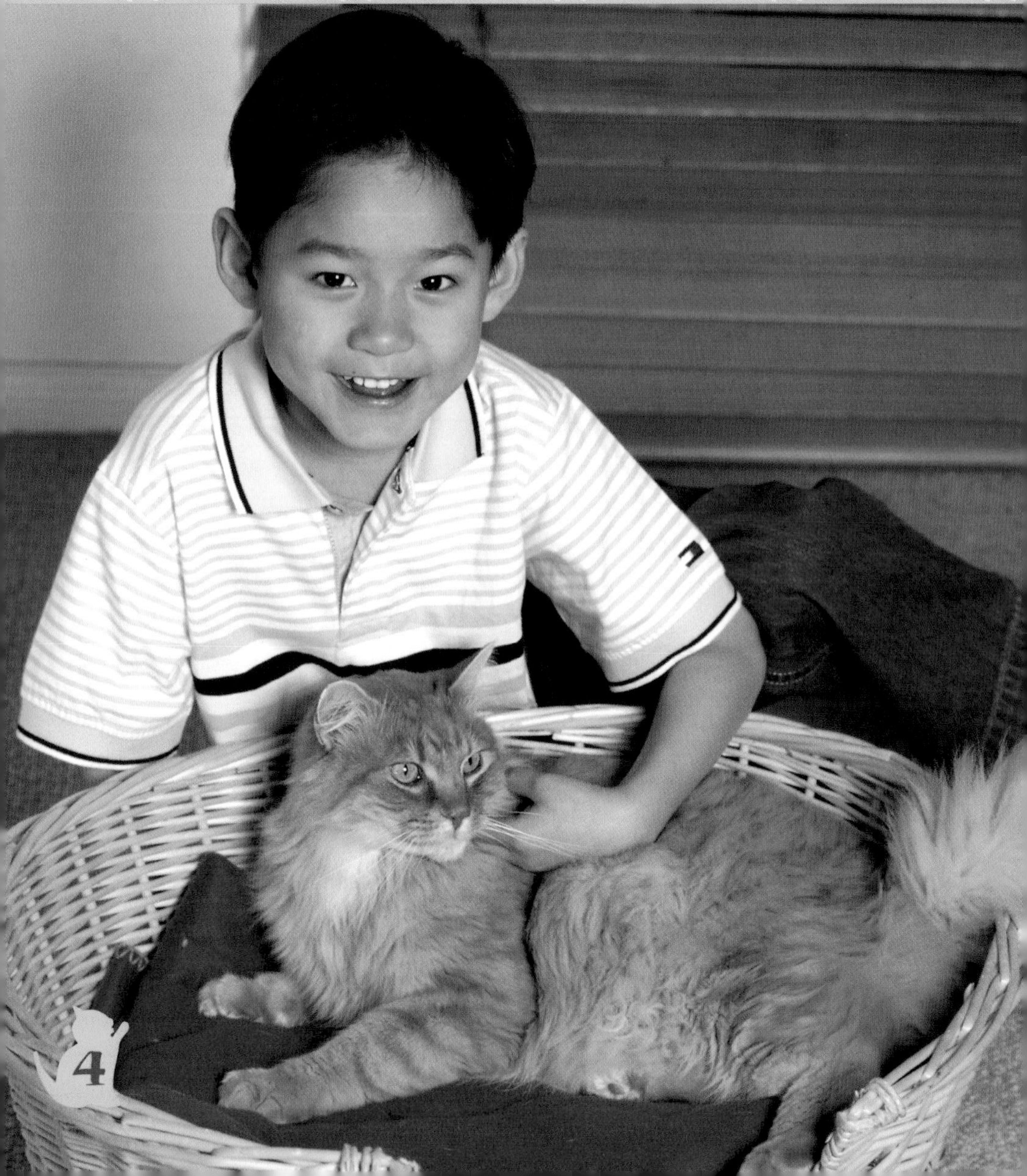

So do I.

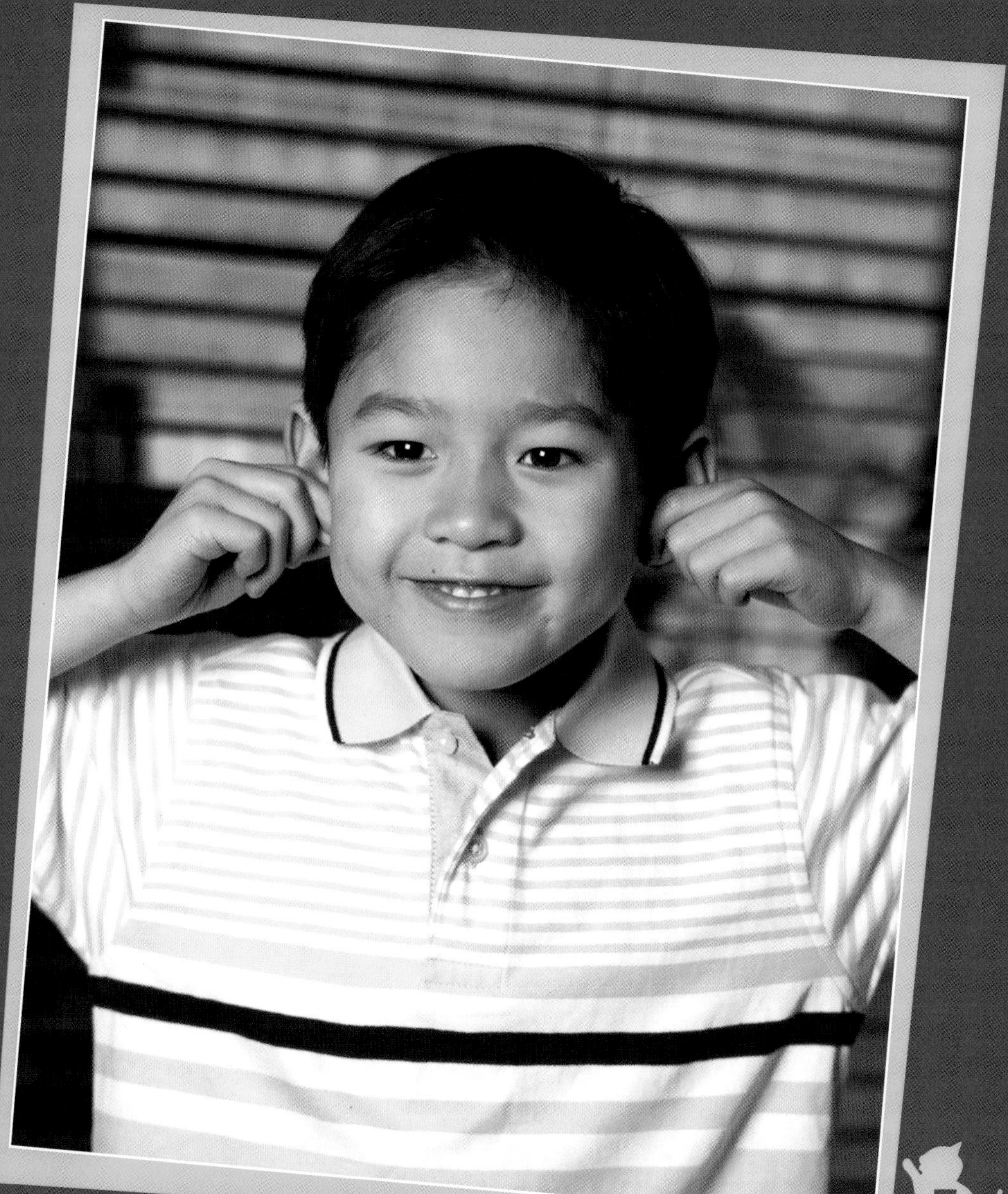

My cat has one nose.

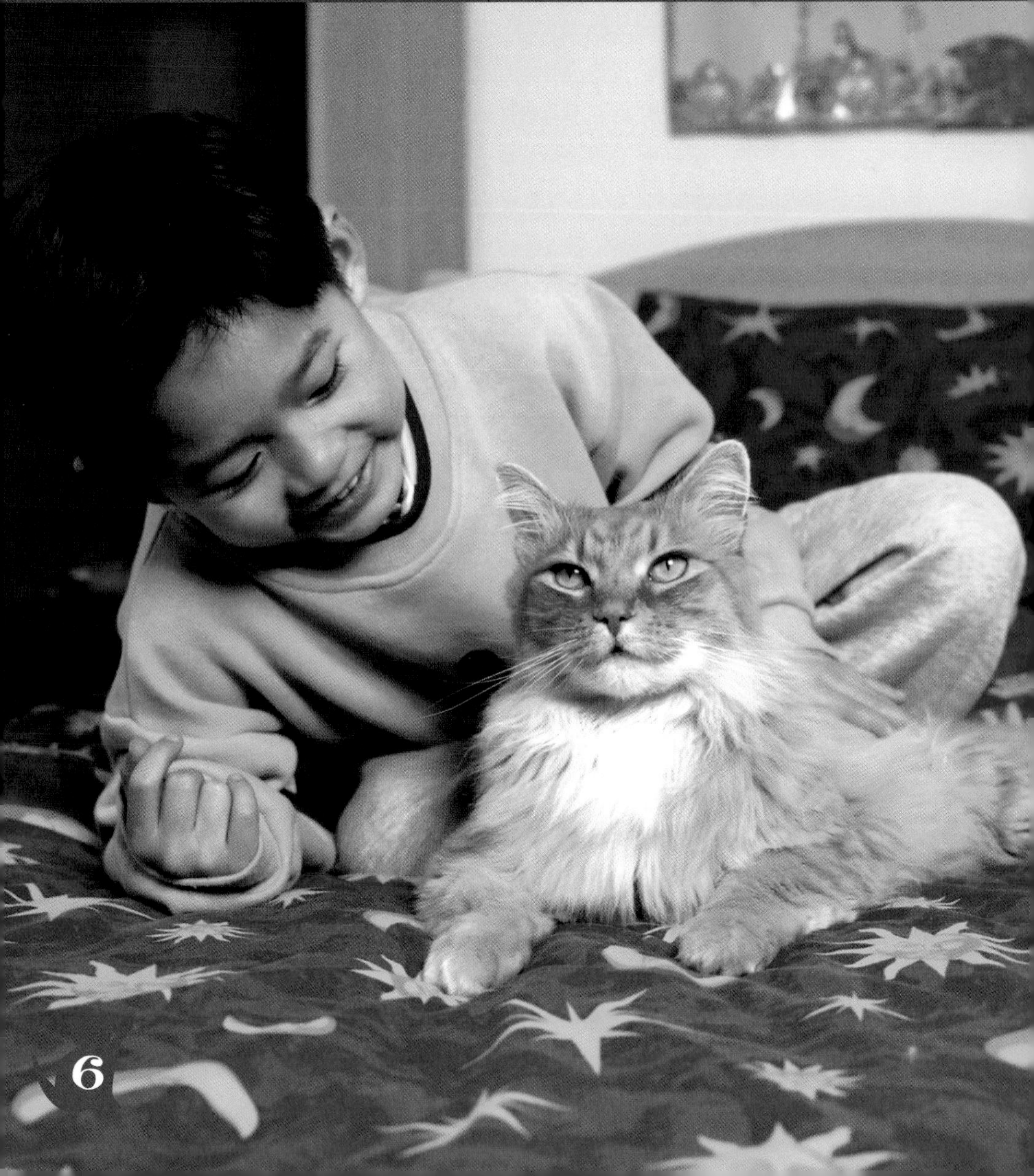

So do I.

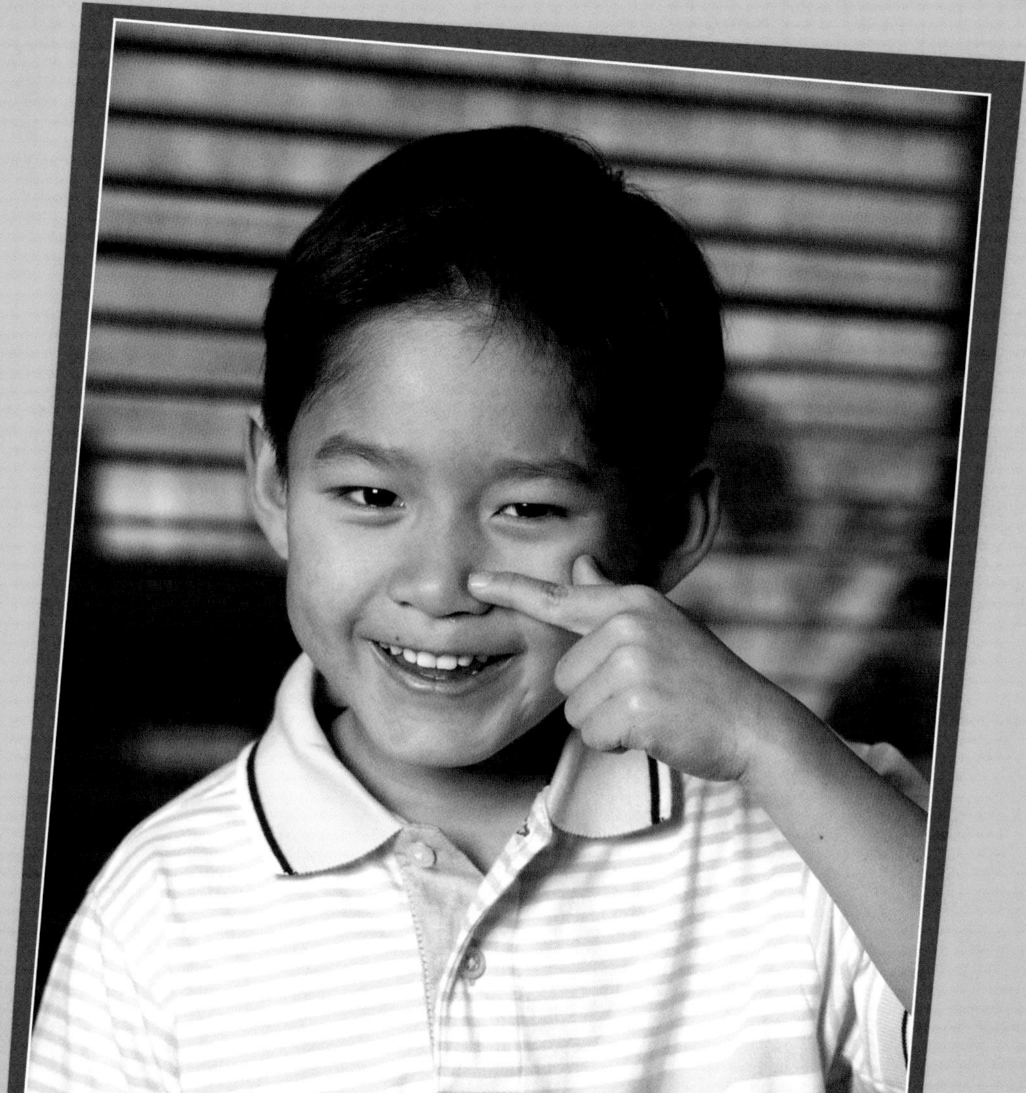

My cat has one tail.
I don't.

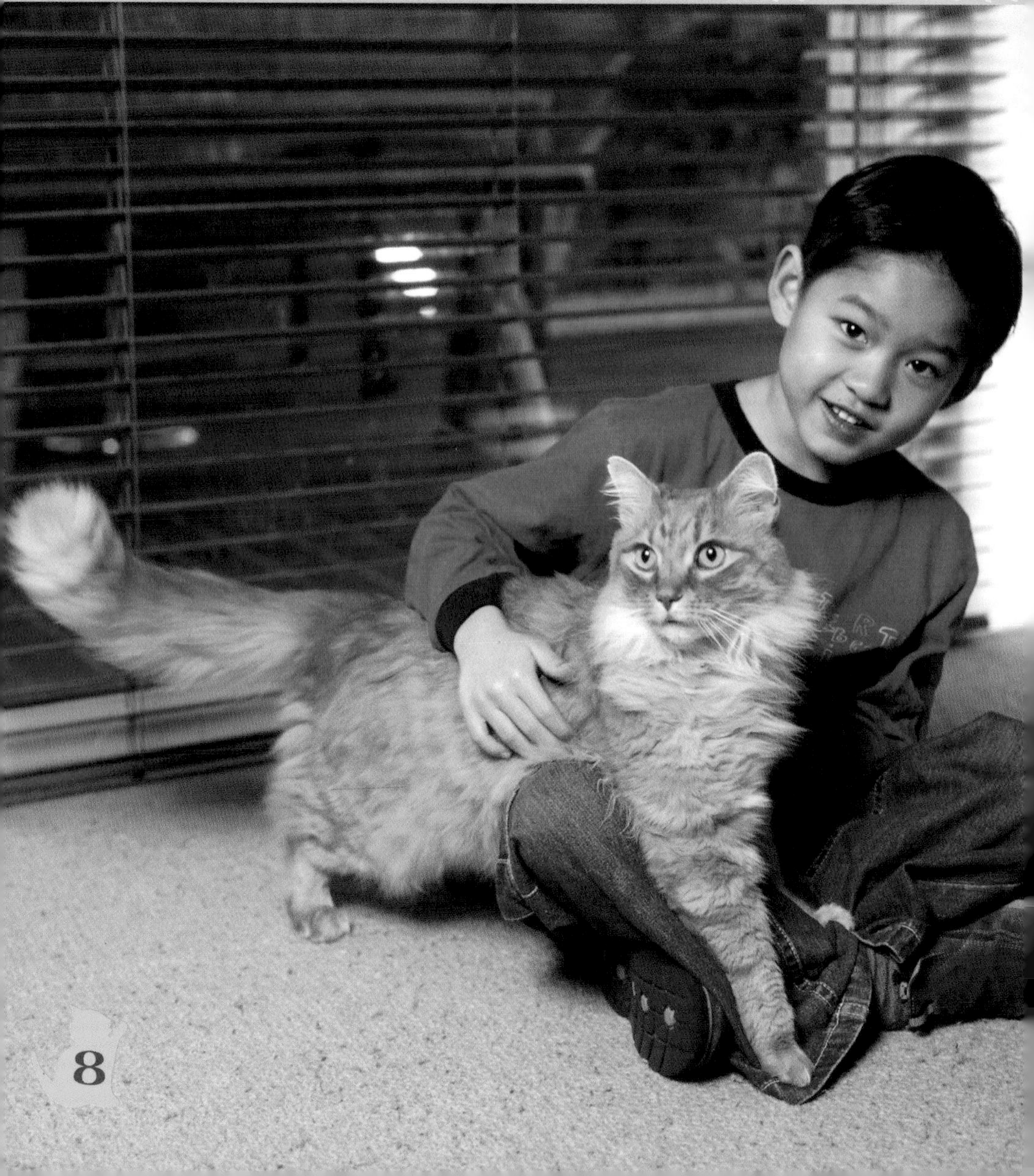